OUR VIETNAM

Tiny Fish Publishing

OUR VIETNAM

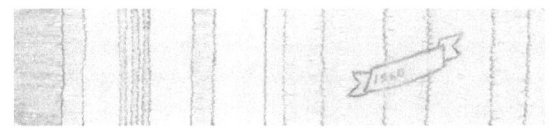

GUY HALL

Hand Illustrated by
MEREDITH HALL

Copyright © 2024 Guy Hall

First published in this form in Australia 2024 by
Tiny Fish Publishing

First published in original form 1999 by
Ginninderra Press

The moral right of the author has been asserted.

All rights reserved.
No part of this publication may be reproduced, distributed, or
transmitted in any form or by any means including photocopying,
recording, storage in a retrieval system or otherwise – except for in the
case of brief quotations embodied in critical articles or reviews –
without the prior written permission of the publisher,
Tiny Fish Publishing.

Paperback ISBN 978-1-7636462-1-6
Ebook ISBN 978-1-7636462-2-3

Illustrations © Meredith Hall
Cover Design © Miriam Diiren
Typesetting by Daiana Morales

Tiny Fish Publishing
P.O Box 997 Norfolk Island NSW 2899
www.tinyfishpublishing.com

 A catalogue record for this book is available from the National Library of Australia

Author's Note

This little book is a collection of deeply personal memories. Although arranged chronologically, they remain separate and distinct memories. As such, I have given each of them their own page. Each deserves that. Some have taken me just a few words to convey, others many. For a few, known only to me, there will never be enough words.

With just one memory per page and some very short, there naturally remains a lot of 'empty' space following those words. That space is for you – to respond however you see fit. You might want to respond with a doodle, a simple sketch, much like Meredith has done with her beautiful pencil drawings. Or you might want to jot down one or two words to express your immediate feelings. Equally, you might simply want to pour out your own heart into that empty space.

In some ways, I like to think of this little book as a conversation – an important one. The part you play in that conversation is central. Despite the (now) many offers of help for veterans and their families, sometimes the most difficult step is having that first conversation. For the children of veterans, that conversation is even more difficult. I know.

My advice to veterans, of any conflict, anywhere in the world, is this: talk to your children. Let them tell you what it was like when you went to war, what it was like when you were away, and what it was like when you eventually came home. I hope that Our Vietnam can help you with that conversation, and many more.

To all those who have picked up this little book, for whatever reason, I trust my journey helps you with yours.

For all those who suffered.

For the future.

And especially for my children.

Come to me in the silence of the night;
Come in the speaking silence of a dream;
Come with soft rounded cheeks and eyes as bright
As sunlight on a stream;
Come back in tears,
O memory, hope, love of finished years.

> Christina Rossetti, 1830 – 1894

Si vis pacem, para bellum.

If you want peace, prepare for war.

> Flavius Vegetius Renatus, AD 379 – 395

Prologue

I was but five months old when, in August of 1962, the Australian Government despatched 30 military advisors to the Republic of Vietnam. When the last Australian serviceman quietly withdrew from Saigon in 1972, over 60,000 Australians had served in Vietnam.

It was a protracted and often unpopular war. But I was the son of a serving Army officer; my perspective was a little different.

These are my memories of our Vietnam.

I

My earliest memory of the war in Vietnam has nothing to do with fighting or suffering. It is of my parents.

When we got home from school, they were there, in the kitchen, standing close together, not saying much. Dad was never home when we got home from school. This day, he was. I don't recall anything else that might have been said. Nor do I remember anything else of that afternoon except the words "Daddy's been sent to Vietnam."

I do remember thinking that this was not a good thing, that there was a war in Vietnam, and that Dad would be away for a long time. To any eight-year-old boy, 'war' doesn't mean a great deal, other than some romantic notions of heroism and guns and stuff. To a soldier's eight-year-old boy, it meant a little more, but I must admit, not a great deal more. I didn't like it, but I don't remember feeling terrified or anything like that. That came later.

II

After that most unusual day, life pretty much returned to 'normal', and I to being an eight-year-old. Time doesn't mean much to one so young – not under normal circumstances anyway.

Dad had learned of his posting to Vietnam some five months before his departure. If I spent five months worrying about it, I have 'gotten over it', for my next memory of Vietnam is of the day he left.

That day is forever creased into my memory; not because a car picked Dad up from home – that had happened before; not because Dad had a lot of big bags packed – he had done that before too. Nor was it because of the obvious – that it was the day my dad went to war. I remember that day as clearly as if it were yesterday, because it was the first time I ever remember seeing my mother cry.

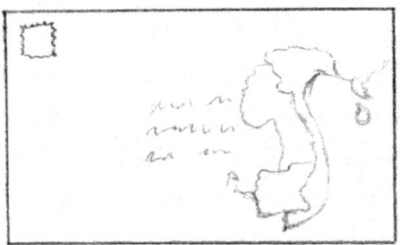

III

Dad kept in constant contact with us. He wrote many letters to us. I can clearly remember the envelope that one such letter came in. It had a map of Vietnam on the front – in blue and white ink. I really had no idea where this place was, other than in Asia somewhere. Some time later, I realised that I had the land and the sea mixed up. I had thought that the blue part was the sea and the white part the land. It was the other way around.

In truth, I had no idea where he was, and I had no idea what he was doing.

IV

Dad also sent many audio tapes to us (the really old sort – reel to reel). To hear his voice was fantastic and when mail arrived that clearly had something in it other than just a letter, I remember all of us being very excited. He told us all sorts of things. He told us what his little hut looked like, what he wore, and how hot it was. I remember him telling us, on one particular tape, how he would sit in the sun outside his hut and feed the lizards that were obviously abundant in Vung Tau. He called them 'his friends'.

We sent tapes back to him, of course. We all told him what we had been up to. I remember telling him how I had gone in Rugby that weekend and how many points I had scored. I thought he would like that.

I don't really remember hearing Mum do her bit.

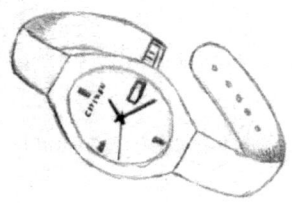

V

Dad had sent the three boys a watch each for Christmas. He had bought them at the US Army 'PX' – the Postal Exchange. They were Citizen watches. It was my first watch. I loved it. I remember telling him on the tape that I wound it every day, although I didn't. Sometimes, I forgot. But I didn't want to tell him that.

VI

The three boys knew where Dad was. He was 'in Vietnam'. I'm sure my eldest brother knew more about it than I did. He was twelve. Our sister, who was only three, didn't know. She was lucky.

I remember feeling very grown up being 'in on it'. I remember feeling very grown up keeping the illusion going for her, telling her, when she asked, that Daddy was away on a 'big job'. We had to pretend that everything was all right.

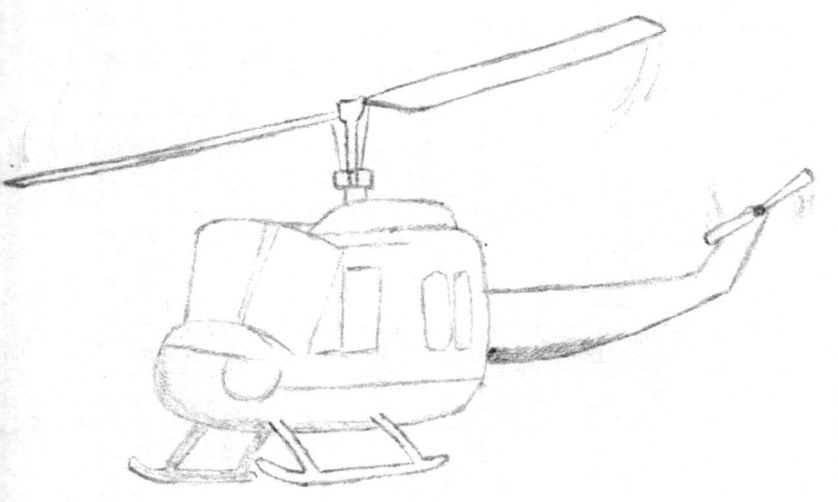

VII

I remember Christmas 1970. In previous years, as children of staff at Royal Military College, we all had an afternoon off school to go to the base Christmas party. What a lark! This year, we didn't, although we still lived on the base at Duntroon. I remember stoically explaining to my schoolmates, who watched the other 'Duntroon kids' heading off for the party, that I wasn't going because "Dad is no longer on staff at RMC." In retrospect, I don't think any of them knew what I was talking about. I don't think that any of them knew that my Dad was in Vietnam. I don't think any of them knew anything about Vietnam.

They did have a Christmas party for us – a special party for the children of soldiers serving in Vietnam. (That was nice, wasn't it?) I remember that there were a lot of kids there. I remember Father Christmas arriving in a helicopter.

I also remember having a turn at sending 'a message to Dad in Vietnam' on film. They had a camera set up there. Mum had said that we could say 'congratulations on your exam results.' (Dad was trying to continue his Uni degree while he was over there!) But I didn't want to say that. I wanted to say 'Dad, I miss you. Come home soon.' So, I did.

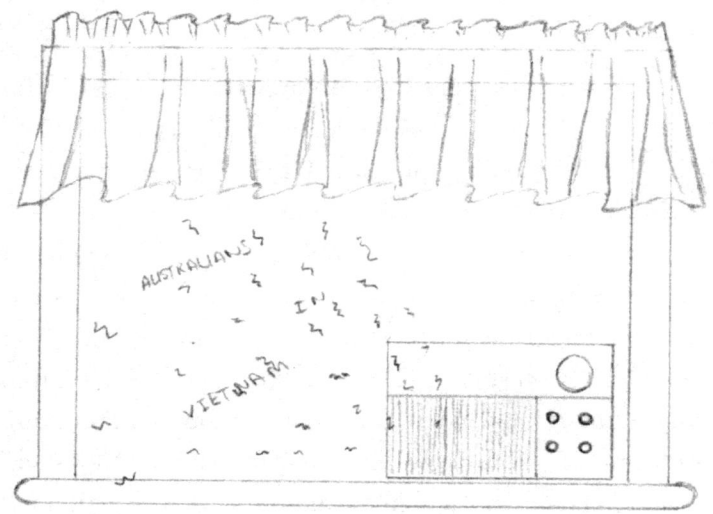

VIII

Mum wouldn't let us listen to the radio much – especially the news. It didn't make much sense at the time. But it didn't really bother me.

However, I can clearly remember the day, and can even remember exactly where I was standing, when I heard one of the news reports that I wasn't supposed to hear: "Another nine Australians have been killed in Vietnam."

I can remember feeling very, very scared. My dad was in Vietnam.

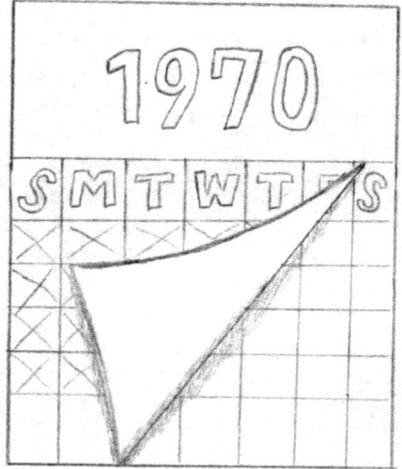

IX

I don't remember much of the next six months. I do remember being very worried and very scared. It was the worst six months of my life.

I also remember feeling that I shouldn't let anybody know that I was scared, especially Mum. A nine-year-old boy doesn't get scared, and if he does, he doesn't show it – and certainly not in front of his school friends. That is how it was supposed to be anyway.

I counted the days until Dad came home.

X

The long-awaited day did come. I remember being a little confused, though. For some reason, the day before Dad was to arrive back in Canberra, Mum went up to Sydney for a night to see him there. She then came home the next morning – ahead of him – and later we all went out to the airport together for his plane to arrive. It wasn't until some years later that I worked that one out! Nine-year-old boys might understand war, but they don't understand everything.

XI

I will never forget when he came home. From inside the terminal, we watched him bounce down the back stairs of the aeroplane. He looked very happy. He looked very young. I remember my little sister, who was now four, rushing away from us through the door marked 'Arrivals' and charging across the tarmac to leap into his arms. It was a great moment. It is a great memory.

XII

I don't remember much more of that day except for going for a walk around Duntroon with Dad and my brother. I remember seeing people rushing out of their front doors and down the little concrete footpaths that all 'married quarters' seemed to have to welcome him home. We were very happy to have him back.

XIII

With Dad home, life again returned to 'normal', although now I watched events in this place 'Vietnam' with a lot more interest and an increasing passion. When my parents sponsored a family of South Vietnamese refugees, I realised that 'this thing' was most certainly not over. I was learning about 'cause and effect'.

The Tran family were lovely people. They seemed very sad, but very happy to be in Australia.

XIV

It was about three years later that I remember making a papier-mâché model of Vung Tau for a school project. Dad helped me with it. He didn't tell me much about the war, although I asked him. (He never talked about it much.) He did seem to enjoy helping me with the model, though. He knew every feature, every detail. He could remember a lot about Vung Tau, Nui Dat, Long Bin and the Phouc Tuoy Province.

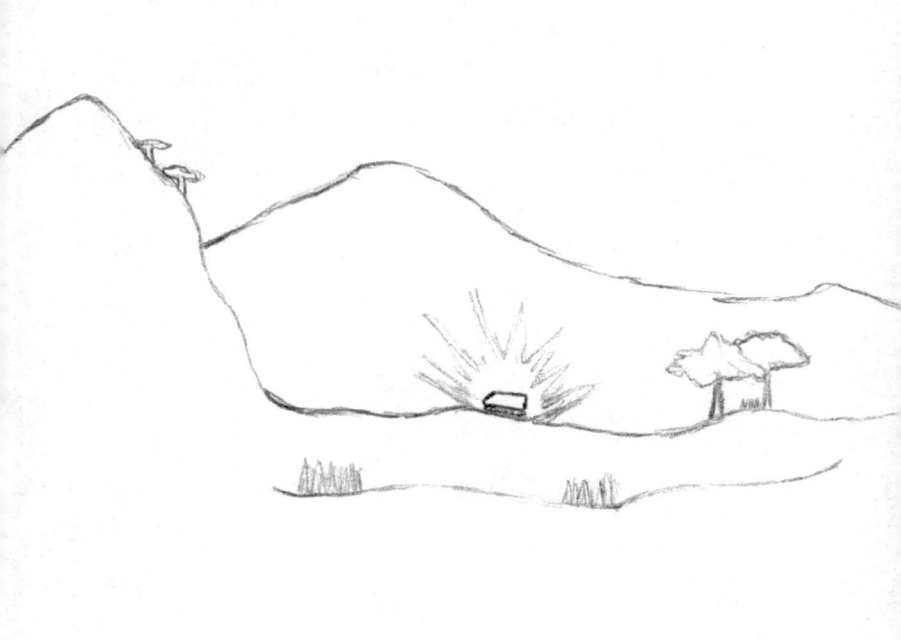

XV

1979: Year 12. I had been working on a compulsory poetry assignment for my Matriculation English class and had shown Dad what I had written. I don't remember what he said (I'm sure that it was something supportive), but what I do remember is that a short time later, he came back to where I was working and handed me a single sheet of paper. On it was a poem that he had written some nine years before – whilst he was in Vietnam.

He didn't tell me a great deal about the circumstances other than that he wrote it after having seen an Armoured Personnel Carrier (an 'APC') destroyed in front of him. He didn't talk much about his feelings – not at all, in fact. I guess he didn't need to. A cry straight from the heart, his poem taught me much about the soldier's Vietnam. It began:

'Far from them, can you feel their war ... ?'

As a child, maybe I hadn't, but I was certainly beginning to...

XVI

In 1980 I entered the Royal Australian Air Force Academy to train as an officer and as a pilot. As a child, of course, I had no idea that that was where I would end up learning my trade. But much had happened over those ten years. Now, I knew that peace did not just happen. Sometimes, it had to be fought for. At all times, it had to be defended – and someone had to defend it.

XVII

We studied many things at RAAF Academy. My degree was in Science – a double major in Physics and Aerodynamics. However, we were also schooled in English, Politics, Economics, military tactics and Australian military history.

We briefly studied the Vietnam War years and their impact on Australian politics and society. I learned, only then, just how bitter the protests really were. (I remember nothing of them at the time. Our mother had protected us well.) I learned about the moratoriums where 'students' and others had sat in roadways and sung their songs. They had wanted the killing to stop. That was fine. So had I. But, some had openly supported the Viet Cong and the North Vietnamese. There were even some who had wanted more Australian soldiers to die – so that the troops would be withdrawn, so that they could make their point; so that they could claim the political and moral high ground. I remember thinking that that was very unfair. Hiding behind their 'morals', these people were hypocrites, cowards and fools.

XVIII

I remember seeing footage of troops returning home from Vietnam. I had often heard my father speak, with a heavy heart, of a particular incident, but I now saw it on film. I watched in horror as a 'peace' protester threw red paint over soldiers marching through the streets of Sydney.

They had called my father a murderer and a 'baby killer'. That had hurt him. He was neither. He was a professional soldier. He was doing his job – protecting them and their country's interests. Above all, he was my dad.

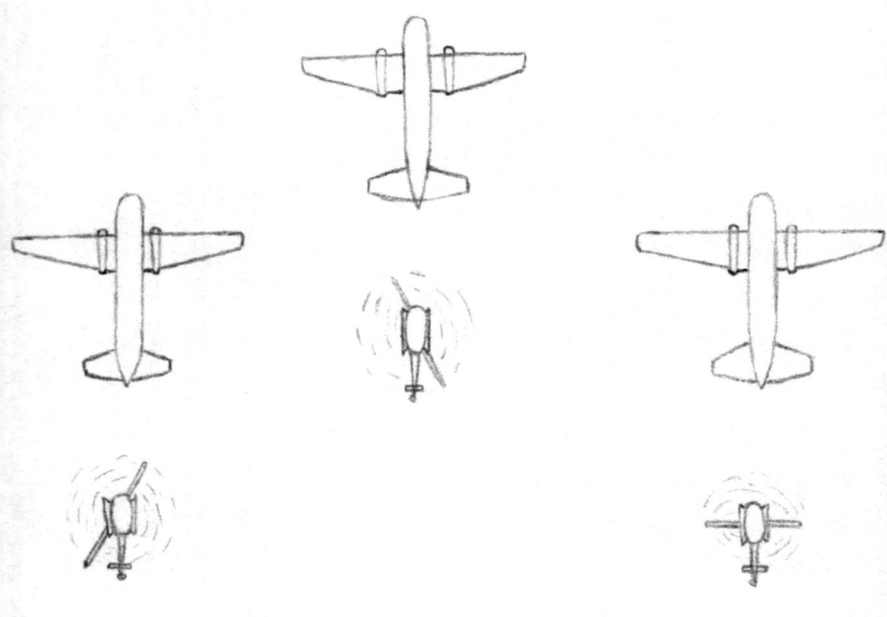

XIX

1987: Twenty-five years after they had first left our shores and travelled into the jungles of Vietnam, and fifteen years since the last returned home, Australia found the maturity and the political will to thank the soldiers for a job well done. They had fought in a war that at times had won little support back home. They had seen and heard their own countrymen and women deriding and vilifying them. They had felt very alone.

There was to be a parade – a welcome home parade – through the streets of Sydney. At last, they could 'come home'.

At the time, I was stationed at the Richmond Air Base, west of Sydney. I was a pilot with 38 Squadron, operating Caribou aircraft – another valiant hero of the war in Vietnam. I rang my father. I asked him (deep inside, I was pleading with him) to come to Sydney and march in his parade. He wasn't ready for that, he had said. He would watch it on TV. So, I offered to march in his stead – it would be my great privilege to represent him there. He accepted, but I still wished that he would come.

But I didn't march. There was to be a flypast of Caribous and Iroquois helicopters – the 'wings' of the Australian soldiers in Vietnam. I eagerly volunteered to lead the formation and, again, I rang my father to tell him, to ask him if that would be okay. As a serving military pilot and the proud son of a veteran, I could think of no better way to show my undying respect for what he had done. The tearful thank-you at the other end of the line will forever remain one of my most cherished memories of our Vietnam.

XX

But I didn't lead the formation either. The Executive Officer of the squadron had himself served in Vietnam as a young Caribou pilot and he, fittingly, would lead the flypast. Having a Vietnam veteran piloting the lead aircraft and another veteran's son 'on his wing' gave our tribute a particularly special touch.

I have never been more emotional in the air than I was on that day. Five hundred and eight Australian flags, one for each Australian killed in Vietnam, led a long overdue parade. Overhead, piloting an aircraft that had been there, a young man honoured and remembered his father, and remembered too, the fear that he might never see him again.

XXI

The following year, Dad marched in the ANZAC Day parade for the first time. He has marched every year since.

XXII

The march in Sydney was a great day for all those who served and suffered in Vietnam. For those who loved them, it was a day long coming, and a welcome one. From that day flowed a river of tears that became a torrent. It was as if the Australian nation had suddenly become aware of how 'unAustralian' it had been to these her sons and daughters, and to those who bore them and loved them.

A memorial was to be built – to be opened in 1992. It would stand on ANZAC Parade in Canberra alongside the other great memorials – to the Australian Light Horse, to the Desert Rats, to the Royal Australian Air Force, to the Australian Naval Forces, and others.

The design of the Vietnam Memorial was, however, to be very different to the other more traditional military memorials. No bronze casts high on marble pillars. No stern, expressionless faces gazing into the future, or the past. This time, things would be different. For a start, there was a lot of ground to make up. There was still a lot of hurt out there.

An essential part of this memorial was to be the participation of the visitor, whether that visitor be one who was there, one of their kin, or a total stranger. They would all be welcome. Crossing over flowing water, three paths lead to the heart of this most moving memorial. Standing at its centre, one cannot be unaffected by the experience that was Vietnam. When you go there, you will know what I mean. Do not hold back your feelings, whatever they may be. They will remain there. They will be accepted there. They will carry you from there.

XXIII

In the forecourt of the Vietnam Memorial, emblazoned in large, bold and perhaps challenging letters is the following:

" For all those who served, suffered and died. "

'It is your memorial as much as it is ours', Dad had said. He knew how much those at home had suffered the Vietnam War. In his view, this memorial was needed as much for them as it was for those who were there. That we were included was very important to him. He brought no pressure to bear, but I felt that he wanted all his children to go there. I think he knew we needed it.

But I knew that he needed it too, and although he marched in the dedication parade, he 'didn't get around' to visiting it afterwards. I spoke to him on the telephone that night. He told me all about the day. In particular, he told me that as he marched, he saw a sign in the crowd. It said: 'My Dad's a Hero'. In tears, I assured him that he had always been my hero. I don't think I'd ever told him that before.

Some weeks later, I again telephoned my father. 'I'll be passing through Canberra again soon', I told him. 'Have you seen the memorial?' he asked. No, I hadn't. Nor had he. He suggested that we go together. I agreed.

So, to our memorial, we took each other. We crossed over the waters and stood at its heart. In silence, we remembered that year, and childhood memories flooded back to me. In silence, we stood and remembered all the years since. We said nothing. We shared much.

Wednesday 15th April 1998.

As I sit for the second night at our dining table watching and talking to my husband as he writes down his memories of Vietnam, I think of my own memories of that time.

Not coming from a family with a military background, my memories are very different.

I remember one of my mother's cousins being of the age for conscription, and I think he was called up and the family being very worried. I seem to remember being very glad that my father couldn't go because he had been discharged medically unfit from National Service some years before. One of his legs was shorter than the other due to a pushbike accident as a young boy. I also remember seeing on the news one night an army tank firing its great big gun. These are my vague memories of the war in Vietnam.

Years later, I met my husband and his father. One afternoon, I was talking to Richard, and he told me something he had only once briefly told Guy. He was sitting on a hill in Vietnam, looking at the beautiful sunset, and he saw one of his Armoured Personnel Carriers going along in the distance. Suddenly, it blew up in front of him. He was remarkably controlled as he told me this. For me, it was a real shock, and I felt such a sadness for the loss of life.

To all the men and women who served in Vietnam, I want to say thank you; and tell you that there are many, many people who respect you for what you did, and are proud of you.

Jo-anne Hall

Far from them, can you feel their war,
or touch their fate as we touch it?
Can you bleed for them as they bleed? -
in brief spurts, that fertilize the sallow
    complexioned soil;
pockmarked with craters of cannonades,
that existed for one moment in eternity
then blew away
with nothing more in their wake
than the minute lumps of flesh
that the diligent or the tearful may collect
and call a body.

                                                       Richard Hall
                                                       12 June 1971

Epilogue

Our Vietnam. Sometimes, it seems like a dream – distant, not quite real. Sometimes, it seems like yesterday, or even today – even this morning. It is that close. My mother's tears, my sister's headlong rush into his arms. At times, I can still feel the fear, the worry, the anger and the joy.

While it is an experience I would not wish on anyone, I have been fortunate, in many ways, to have 'been there'. While I can never know my father's Vietnam, our Vietnam has taught me much about many things.

ABOUT US.

The Author: Guy Hall

Guy was born in Melbourne but, as the son of a soldier, grew up in various places in Australia and the United States of America.

He graduated from the Royal Australian Air Force Academy in 1983 and flew as an operational Air Force pilot and Qualified Flying Instructor until 1990, when he joined Australian Airlines, then Qantas Airways in 1994.

Now semi-retired, he and his wife Jo-anne share their time between homes on Norfolk Island and Melbourne where their five children live and work.

Guy is both excited and honoured to re-publish *Our Vietnam* in collaboration with two of his children, Meredith and Miriam.

'Guy has that rare ability to evoke depth with few words.'

> Maj Gen Peter Phillips
> Vietnam War veteran
> National President of RSL 1997 – 2003

The Illustrator: Meredith Hall

Meredith lives in Melbourne, Australia. She is a Fashion Designer by trade where hand drawing remains a key skill. Her preferred medium is pencil, as it allows her to capture mood as well as fine detail. This is her first book illustration.

The Cover Designer: Miriam Diiren (nee Hall)

Also from Melbourne, Miriam is a Communication Designer by profession working in the creative marketing space. This is her first book cover design.

Front Cover
The front cover illustration is a stylised representation of the Vietnam War memorial in ANZAC Parade, Canberra.

The two military ribbons represent the Australian Vietnam Medal and the Republic of Vietnam Campaign Medal.

Back Cover
Photograph of the author, aged 9 years, 1971.

A final thought for the journey. If you need to talk...

In Australia:

Open Arms – Veterans and Families counselling.

A service founded by Vietnam Veterans, now for all veterans and families, provides free and confidential counselling 24/7 to partners and children of those who have served.
    1800 011 046
    https://www.openarms.gov.au/

Department of Veterans' Affairs – Mental health support services.

If you have served at least one day in the Australian Defence Force (ADF), including reservists, several options are available to support your mental health and well-being.
    1800 628 036
    https://www.dva.gov.au/get-support/

Lifeline – 24/7 crisis support.

A national charity providing all Australians experiencing emotional distress with access to 24-hour crisis support and suicide prevention services. A safe place to be heard.
    13 11 14
    https://www.lifeline.org.au/

Beyond Blue – 24/7 qualified support.

Helping all Australians achieve their best possible mental health. Earlier, easier together.
    1300 224 636
    https://www.beyondblue.org.au/

Internationally:

HelpGuide.org

A handy search tool to find Mental Health helplines in any country.
    https://www.helpguide.org/find-help

www.ingramcontent.com/pod-product-compliance
Lightning Source LLC
Chambersburg PA
CBHW060346080526
44583CB00014B/1083